THE
BOOK OF
GRACE

Books by Suzan-Lori Parks
Available from TCG

The America Play and Other Works
Also Includes:
Betting on the Dust Commander
The Death of the Last Black Man in the Whole Entire World
Devotees in the Garden of Love
Imperceptible Mutabilities in the Third Kingdom
Pickling
Essays

The Book of Grace

Father Comes Home from the Wars (Parts 1, 2 & 3)

The Red Letter Plays
Includes:
Fucking A
In the Blood

365 Days/365 Plays

Topdog/Underdog

Venus

THE BOOK OF GRACE

SUZAN-LORI PARKS

Theatre Communications Group
New York
2016

The Book of Grace is published by Theatre Communications Group, Inc., 520 Eighth Avenue, 24th Floor, New York, NY 10018-4156

The publication of *The Book of Grace*, by Suzan-Lori Parks, through TCG's Book Program, is made possible in part by the New York State Council on the Arts with the support of Governor Andrew Cuomo and the New York State Legislature.

Special thanks to Paula Marie Black for her generous support of this publication.

TCG books are exclusively distributed to the book trade by Consortium Book Sales and Distribution.

Library of Congress Cataloging-in-Publication Data

Parks, Suzan-Lori.
The book of grace / Suzan-Lori Parks.
pages ; cm
ISBN 978-1-55936-405-8 (paperback)
ISBN 978-1-55936-646-5 (ebook)
1. Fathers and sons—Texas—Drama. I. Title.
PS3566.A736B66   2015
812'.54—dc23   2014044577

Book design and composition by Lisa Govan
Cover painting and design by Rodrigo Corral Studio/June Park

First Edition, January 2016

For Buddy

And for Stephanie Ellen

THE
BOOK OF
GRACE

Production History

The Book of Grace had its world premiere at The Public Theater (Oskar Eustis, Artistic Director; Andrew D. Hamingson, Executive Director) in New York on March 17, 2010. It was directed by James Macdonald; the set design was by Eugene Lee, the costume design was by Susan Hilferty, the lighting design was by Jean Kalman, the sound design was by Dan Moses Schreier, the projection/video design was by Jeff Sugg; the dramaturg was John Dias and the production stage manager was Amy McCraney. The cast was:

Vet	John Doman
Buddy	Amari Cheatom
Grace	Elizabeth Marvel

The Book of Grace opened at ZACH Theatre (Dave Steakley, Producing Artistic Director; Elisbeth Challener, Managing Director) in Austin, Texas, on June 4, 2011. It was directed by the author; the set and costume design were by Michael Raiford, the lighting design was by Jason Amato, the sound design was by Antonio Garfias, the video design was by Colin Lowry; the stage mangers were Ian Scott and Carmela Valdez. The cast was:

Vet	Eugene Lee
Buddy	Shaun Patrick Tubbs
Grace	Nadine Mozon

Author's Note on the Productions

A Whole Can of Worms

In NYC, at The Public, we worked with a superb multiracial cast. In Austin, at ZACH, we worked with an equally superb cast, and chose to go ABC (All Black Casting). I feel that a monochromatic casting allows the production to embrace the more profound and thorny themes of the play. That said, I also understand that any casting choice will, especially with this play, open up its own can of worms.

Characters

Vet
Buddy
Grace

Setting

A house in a small town near the Border.

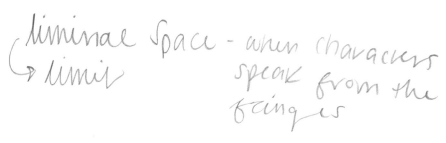

liminal space – when characters speak from the fringes → limit

From the Author's Elements of Style

I'm continuing the use of my slightly unconventional theatrical elements. Here's a road map.

- *(Rest)*
  Take a little time, a pause, a breather; make a transition.

- A Spell
  An elongated and heightened *(Rest)*. Denoted by repetition of figures' names with no dialogue. Has sort of an architectural look:

  Buddy
  Vet
  Buddy
  Vet

  This is a place where the figures experience their pure true simple state. While no action or stage business is necessary, directors should fill this moment as they best see fit.

- ((Parentheses around dialogue indicate softly spoken passages—asides; sotto voce.))

- [[Brackets indicate possible cuts for production.]]

Prologue

Vet, standing outside near the Border Fence, wearing his uniform
and, with his binoculars, scanning the horizon.
Grace, in her kitchen, wearing her waitress uniform,
and holding her red-marbled composition book, her *Book of Grace*.
Buddy, outside, in a no-man's land, wearing t-shirt and jeans
with a keychain on his belt. He's got his footlocker
and a full-to-bursting plastic shopping bag.

Vet
Buddy
Grace

(Rest)

Grace
There's a lot of good in the world

Vet
It's all about Us and Them

Buddy
I can't forgive what he's done. What he's done to me. No way

Grace

You just gotta look for it. The good. You just gotta look

Vet

That's why Borders are good. They keep us contained

Buddy

I can't forget it, but I could forgive it. Forgiving it will depend on him

Grace

Sure there's bad. But there's good too. Like

Vet

Borders keep Us on our side and Them on theirs. And that's a good

Buddy

Forgiving it will depend on him not forgetting it. Funny how that works, huh?

Grace

Like that baby hippo and that old turtle. They're friends. That's good

Vet

And that's a good thing. Borders

Buddy

I can't forget it

Grace

Like the man who saved the lady when she fell into the river. He risked his own life to do it. That's good

Vet

Borders and Fences, they say it all without saying a word: that is yours and this is mine

Buddy

I can't forget it

Grace
Why did he save her from drowning? Cause something in him was leaning toward the good

Buddy
I can't forget it. Ok?

Vet
I see an Illegal trying to get in here and I say, "Stop in the name of the U.S. Border Patrol." That's my job

Buddy
He's my "father." I use that term loosely. Let me be specific: he is my very own motherfucker

Grace
There's so much evidence of good. So I write it down in my book.

Buddy
I'm Buddy, Pop. Here I am. This is how I turned out

Vet
I have contained myself. I've changed. I'm on the good foot now

Buddy
Unspeakable. The things he did to me

Vet
He'll try to make me admit to stuff

Buddy
Unspeakable

Grace
Looking on the bright side doesn't cost nothing

Buddy
It can't be forgot but it can be forgiven

Vet
I've contained myself

Buddy
Three chances he'll get. Three strikes: 1-2-3

Vet
I've contained myself

Buddy
Hey, I am, after all, his son

Grace
You just gotta look for it. The good. The good is all around

Vet
Buddy
Grace

(Rest)

> Reading from her Book:

Grace
The Book of Grace.
(Rest)

> A bell, thumb-cymbal sounding, rings.
> As the lights change, Buddy hides his plastic bag. He hides it
> somewhere in the audience—silently asking folks to keep his secret.

Chapter 47

Early morning. A small one-bedroom house. Fairly well kept.
Reading from her Book:

Grace
The Book of Grace, Chapter 47: Aliens.

Vet, working on his speech, recites while watching the tv
and ironing his green uniform. He finishes one
and begins ironing another.

Vet
"Aliens. That's what we're up against. Aliens. Not the ones
from outer space although they might be. Although they
could be. From another planet. From another land. Their
land might as well be another planet. Because they're
strange. They're not like us. That's why we've got to keep
them out. And a Border alone won't do it. That's why the
Fence, the Border Fence, that's why it's a miracle. The
Border Fence is a modern miracle."
(Rest)
Yeah. That's it. Keep it simple. It's a speech. Talk about
something they can all understand.
(Rest)

"This here. This is a crease. They see these creases and they know they're done for. We all wear the uniform. And we wear it proudly. Sometimes I even sleep in mine."

(Rest)

No, don't tell them that.

(Rest)

"This crease makes a Fence all its own."

(Rest)

(Rest)

"I caught those Illegals and their truckload of drugs and I did it single-handedly. So now I'm getting a medal for it. And I thank you."

(Rest)

"Aliens. Sometimes the Alien is right in your own home. Sometimes right in your own blood. And you've got to build a wall around it."

(Rest)

Maybe not that part but the first part. Yeah. Ok. Lead with Aliens then keep it down to earth. All right.

He continues ironing.

Chapter 48

> Some time later. Vet still ironing. Tv still on.
> Reading from her Book:

Grace
The Book of Grace, Chapter 48: My Version of Homeland Security.

> Buddy, standing in the doorway with his footlocker.
> He wears t-shirt and jeans.

Buddy
I've got I.D. Identification.

Vet
That's good.

Buddy
You need to see it?

Vet
Are you really Buddy?

Buddy
Sure, Pop.

Vet
Just asking.

Buddy
I've got I.D. Take a look.
(Rest)
I'll put it right here.

> Buddy sets his identification card down and glances at the tv.
> Vet joins him.

Vet
The Border Fence. There it is.

Buddy
That's where you work.

Vet
That's right.

Buddy
"Border Patrol Officer single-handedly catches 8 Illegal Immigrants and their truckload of drugs."

Vet
You saw the news.

Buddy
I knew it was you before they said your name.

Vet
You recognized me. I've changed a lot.

Buddy
Me too.

Vet
For better or for worse?

Buddy
That's a frame-of-reference question.

Vet
How long you planning on staying?

Buddy
Just for your Ceremony.

Vet
That's tomorrow.

Buddy
So I'll just stay the night.

Vet
Grace says you might stay longer.

Buddy
She home?

Vet
She's at work.
(Rest)
I say we'll see.

Buddy
About what?

Vet
About you staying longer. We expected you yesterday.

Buddy
I got held up.

Vet
Grace baked you a cake. She wanted to have a party.

Buddy
Yeah, she said.

Vet
She said?

Buddy
In her letter. I sent her a picture—

Vet
—She showed me—

Buddy
—So she'd know it was me. So you would too.

Vet
It's been a while. 10 years.

Buddy
15 years.

Vet
Point taken.

Buddy
I got an honorable discharge. A few years ago.

Vet
And you've just been doing what since then? Just kicking around?

Buddy
Pretty much.
(Rest)
Can I get some water?

Vet
Hold up.

           Vet approaches Buddy. Buddy raises his arms.

Vet
My version of Homeland Security. On the job and at home too.

           Buddy submits to Vet's thorough pat-down. Vet takes Buddy's
                  phone from his pocket. Looks it over.

Vet

You've got one of these, huh? A *Smartphone*.

Buddy

It's a few years old.

> Vet hands the phone back.

Vet

You believe in the right to bear arms?

Buddy

Sure. For self-protection. But I don't got a gun.

Vet

Do you want one?

Buddy

Not right now.

Vet

You're not a liberal?

Buddy

No, sir.

Vet

Good. There's the sink. Help yourself.

> Vet goes back to his ironing and also watches as
> Buddy goes to the sink, getting a few handfuls of water.

Vet

This heat makes me think of ice cream. Remember that time
I took you for ice cream?

Buddy

No.

Vet

We had black walnut. My favorite.

Buddy
Ok.

Vet
I got a single. You got a double-dip.

Buddy
Triple-dip.

Vet
So you remember. You got a favorite anything?

Buddy
Nope.

Vet
That ice cream was almost as big as you.

Buddy
Almost.

Vet
And your mother got vanilla.

Buddy
Strawberry.

Vet
Right.
(Rest)
Too bad she passed.

Buddy
No one at her funeral but me. You could of come.

Vet
What for?

Buddy
Right. I got the condolence card Grace sent. I guess me visiting here was all her idea, right?

Vet
The card was from both of us. And you visiting: we thought of it together.

Buddy
Right.

Grace
Footnote #1:

> Grace, waitressing at the diner,
> pauses from her work to speak to us.

Grace
So I said to him, "Vet, don't look at me like I'm crazy. You're getting a medal, he's got a medal already. You're doing pretty good, he's doing pretty good. It's the perfect time for you and Buddy to see each other again. You say you 'can't see him.' But you've got eyes, don't you? Of course you do. So you'll see him and you two will make amends. It'll be good for both of you. No brainer."

Buddy
That Fence. It's something.

> Buddy watches the tv. Vet watches Buddy.

Vet
That's live-streaming video. But even live-streaming video doesn't do it justice.

Buddy
Maybe you'll take me to see it.

Vet
You'll see it tomorrow at the Ceremony with everybody else.
(Rest)
Grace says you're looking for work. She thinks you should work Patrol. With me.

Buddy

There's a fast-track for military guys.

Vet

But I'm guessing you've had a few blemishes on your record since you got out.

Buddy

Nothing too serious.

Vet

Still, you'll need my good word to smooth your path.

Buddy

Yeah. I would.

Buddy
Vet

(Rest)

Buddy

I got a favorite tree.

Vet

Ok.

Buddy

The one we had in the yard on Myrtle Avenue was pretty good.

Vet

Pine.

Buddy

Elm.

Vet

It was pine, I'm telling you.

Buddy

When we lived on Elm Street we had a pine tree, but on Myrtle Ave we had the elm. But that was just me and Mom, when we lived on Myrtle.

Vet

Right.

Buddy

So you probably wouldn't remember it. The elm.

Vet

That pine tree was something though, wasn't it? You practically lived up there. And then when that cone fell down and popped you on the head you took it personal. Stuck your firecrackers around the trunk and tried to blow it up.

Buddy

I almost did too.

Vet

Fire department had to come. Your mother blamed it on me.

Buddy

Yeah.
(Rest)
When's Grace coming home?

Vet

In a couple of hours. She's at work, or at least that's where she says she is.
(Rest)
You're grown and I'm old. Is that what you're thinking?

Buddy

You're working that iron pretty good.

Vet

50 push-ups, 200 sit-ups every morning.

Buddy
I do twice that.

Vet
Want me to call Grace?

Buddy
No need.

Vet
You two talk on the phone a lot?

Buddy
Nope.

Vet
Just letters? Emails?

Buddy
Just letters.
(Rest)
You wear Kevlar?

Vet
Why you asking?

Buddy
Just making conversation.

Vet
A bullet-proof vest? We could, but the job doesn't go that way too often. Most Tonks don't hardly got shoes let alone a gun. Although I've got mine. Glock.

Buddy
They make you keep it locked up at the station?

Vet
They don't make me. That's my decision. Keeps things— contained.

Buddy
You have changed.

Vet
Yep.

Buddy
You keep that Fence on all day?

Vet
It feeds to the tv. From the "interwebs." So we can monitor the Border 24/7. Grace says I shouldn't bring my work home with me. The live-feed's mostly for volunteers, but I like it too.

Buddy
It's interesting.

Vet
You want a beer? I know it's early, but—

> Vet takes two beers from the fridge, hands one to Buddy
> who holds up his hand in refusal.

Buddy
I'm all right.

Vet
I could put an egg in it. Make it breakfast.

Buddy
No thanks.

Vet
Not your brand? It's American. The can's red-white-and-blue at least.

Buddy
I don't drink.

Vet
You drink water.

Buddy
Not spirits.

Vet
You a Muslim?

Buddy
Nope.

Vet
Next thing I know you'll drop down and be praying on the rug.
East is that way, if you're wondering.

Buddy
I'm not.

Vet
So you're a 12-Stepper?

Buddy
Nope.

Vet
Just a Teetotaler. Ok. Your mother inhabited the opposing
camp on the subject of drinking if I remember correctly. I'm
easy on the spirits. So you're like me.

Buddy
I guess.

Vet
You're easy on the spirits, I'm easy on the spirits. We believe
in the same things. You got a footlocker. I got a footlocker.
I got private stuff in mine. What's in yours?

Buddy
Private stuff.

Vet
We're 2 peas in a pod. You turned out all right. Pretty much.

Buddy
Thanks.

Vet
Ceremony's going to be a social situation. Around here if you don't at least hold a beer in your hand, people will think twice about you. Then they'll think twice about me.

> Buddy picks up the unopened beer and holds it.

Buddy
Should I open it?

Vet
If we were in a social situation.

Buddy
We're not in a social situation?

Vet
No, Buddy, we're at home.

Buddy
Your home, not mine.

Vet
My home and we're glad you're here.

Grace
Footnote #2:

> Again, Grace pauses from her work.

Grace
And then I told him, "Vet, you'll know what to say. Say 'welcome home.' Ok, so it's not his home. Say 'we're glad you're here.' Offer him a beer and a seat, Vet. It's not brain surgery. Or is it? Ok, maybe it is brain surgery. Better get out your rubber gloves. No, don't get out your rubber gloves, Vet. Just offer him a beer and tell him to sit down. Forgive and forget. I mean, how bad can it be, right?"

Vet

Grace wants you to stay. Longer than just the night. Christ, the things she's got going on in her head. She's thinking, together, the three of us can be some sort of family unit: me the Father, you the Son and her as the—Holy Ghost.

> They enjoy that together.

Vet	**Buddy**
(Rest)	
Stupid-dumb.	Stupid-dumb. I remember that. You and Grace? Kids?

Vet

Nope.

> Vet's finished ironing. He would go into the bedroom to change,
> but, to keep his eye on
> Buddy, he stays in the room, getting dressed.

Vet

Look at that crease. Grace, she can't understand the importance of a good crease. It's just a boundary, just a line of demarcation. But that kind of understanding is beyond her. She came home one day. Reading one of those women's magazines and took one of the tests they've got in there, counted up her score and says the test says that she's got "boundary issues." Well, I could of told her that.

> Buddy is looking out the window.

Buddy

It's nice here. Nice house. Nice yard.

Vet

At night you can see the Fence from here. And when I'm over there I can see the house. From there, we're the closest lights in the distance. They wanted me to live on the base, with everybody else, but I don't like people in my business.

Buddy

What's the hole in the backyard for?

Vet
Buddy

(Rest)

Vet

How was the Service?

Buddy

I qualified as "expert" on the M-16. I worked the M-79 for a while.

Vet

Grenade launcher.

Buddy

Yeah. I got out and I took some classes. A government class. "When in the course of human events it becomes necessary—"

Vet

No need to school me.

Buddy

I know the whole thing. The Constitution too.

Vet

Grace said you were mostly a sort of army waterboy.

Buddy

Water Transport Specialist.

Vet

Ok.

Buddy

I got promoted. Got working as a Combat Engineer too. Building anti-tank ditches, laying landmines.

Vet

Blowing up stuff. Ok. You put your childhood inclination to good use.

Buddy

I got the Bronze Star too.

Vet

Tell the truth, now.

> Buddy takes off his boot.
> Empties out his medal.
> Shows it to Vet.

Vet

Might as well take off the other one too.

> Buddy takes off his other boot. Shakes it out. Nothing in it.

Vet

Where's your name?

Buddy

They don't put your name on it. It's like the Olympics. You get a medal in the Olympics they don't put your name on it.

Vet

Grace would say we're finding our "Common Ground."
(Rest)
I'm getting a medal too. The Governor's coming down. The whole town will be there. The local news crew. The marching band. They're telling me I'll have to give a speech.

Buddy

A speech?

Vet

Yeah.

Buddy

What's the hole in the backyard for?

Vet
It's a deterrent.

Buddy
You said you changed.

Vet
Grace says I'm a work-in-progress.

Buddy
What do you say?

Vet
I say, are you in trouble?

Buddy
In trouble? No, sir.

Vet
Except for your stint in the Service you were always in trouble. Are you in trouble now?

Buddy
I'm doing great.

Vet
Mind if I take a look?

Buddy
Yes.

Vet
I've probably got a key that could fit it.

Buddy
Vet

> Buddy unlocks his footlocker, opening the lid. Vet puts on some
> latex gloves before gently looking through the contents.
> Some bric-a-brac, old clothes, not much else.

Buddy
Just some old junk from Mom's house.

Vet
Too bad you lost it.

Buddy
They took it.

Vet
Well if you don't pay the bill, they'll do that.

Buddy
I could use a job.

Vet
We'll see.

Buddy
I need to get back on my feet. It's been hard.

Vet
I said we'll see.

Buddy
We'll see.
(Rest)
Unspeakable. The things you did to me.

Vet
I don't know what you're talking about.

Buddy
Maybe we should just forget it.

Vet
I don't know what you're talking about. What I do know is:
I'm on the good foot now. Past behind me. Future in front.
Like it should be, ok? Ok. Hey, ok, maybe I'll have time later
tonight. I could show you the Fence. See the Fence, meet the
guys. Even a job—maybe.

Buddy
"Maybe."

Vet
You should get a haircut. So when you meet the guys you'll look correct. There's a barbershop—

Buddy
You really don't have any recollection of it?

Vet
It's past. I'm living today, ok?

Buddy
Vet
Buddy

> Buddy holds up his thumb, like he's counting. It's Strike One.

Vet
What's that for?

Buddy
I hitchhiked. From the bus stop.

> Buddy stands there with his thumb still extended.
> Vet looks at the clock on the wall and then at his watch.
> He goes to the house phone, making a call.

Vet
Time at the tone is a real lifesaver.

> He resets the clock, then his watch.

Vet
Past behind, future in front. All right?

Buddy
We'll see.

He's still got his thumb out, but not brandishing it so obviously.

Vet
Well—"Welcome home, Buddy." I'll swing by the barbershop later. Pick you up if you're there. Then we could do the tour.

Buddy
Sure.

> Vet goes.
> Buddy stands there watching the Fence on tv.
> The sound of Vet's truck fades into the distance.
> When the coast is clear, Buddy goes outside
> and retrieves his plastic bag.
> Back in the house he opens his footlocker and transfers the bag's
> contents: several Army-issue hand grenades:
> very precious, very dangerous.

Buddy
Strike One.

Chapter 49

A few hours later.
Grace just home from work. She wears her waitress uniform
and carries old newspapers.

Grace
The Book of Grace, Chapter 49: Buddy. Grace. Right.

Buddy sleeps on the couch. She stands there looking at him.

Grace
Buddy
Grace
Buddy

(Rest)

She gets a closer look at his face. He doesn't wake.
She sits on the edge of the couch, looking at him.
Buddy fidgets in his sleep. She keeps staring at him.

Grace
Grace
Grace
Grace

Grace
Grace
Grace
Grace

> She scrounges around in her purse, pulling out a waitress notepad.
> Scrounges around for a pen.
> Scribbles something on the pad. A fresh page,
> another glance at Buddy, then more scribbling.
> A glance at Buddy's footlocker.
> Buddy gently wakes and watches her. She's absorbed and doesn't
> notice at first. When she does, she hops up,
> dropping her notepad, then toeing it under the couch.

Grace
Buddy!

Buddy
Grace.

Grace
Right.

Buddy
Well, hey.

Grace
Hey.

Buddy
Grace
Buddy
Grace

> They hug gently and then separate.

Grace
15 years.

Buddy
Yeah.

Grace
You got here!

Buddy
I did.

Grace
Right on.

Buddy
I guess.

Grace
And you've come back to help celebrate your dad. Gold Star,
Buddy.

Buddy
Grace

Grace
What?

Buddy
Nothing.

Grace
Tell me.

Buddy
No thanks.

Buddy
Grace
Buddy
Grace
Buddy
Grace

The distance between them feels like miles.

Chapter 50

As Buddy and Grace are squaring off in the living room, Vet, wearing his gun, is at work. He scans the horizon with his binoculars. He's still figuring out his speech.

Grace

The Book of Grace, Chapter 50: Marginalia: Sometimes I Don't See Anything.

Vet

"Sometimes I don't see anything. Sometimes I can stand here for hours and look and look and—what am I looking at? The Fence. And nothing. The dirt. The rocks. The sand. The gophers. The lizards. The jackalopes. Just kidding. No such thing as a jackalope. No such thing as an honest Illegal. Honest Illegal is a whatchacallit. An oxymoron. Oxymoron. Funny word. If I didn't speak English I'd think that meant— 'clean idiot.' Most of them don't speak English."
(Rest)
You're rambling. Your speech isn't a speech yet, it's a ramble. A babble. A wander. Give them something more substantial, Vet. Put the job in a nutshell.
(Rest)

¡SAL DEL COCHE! ¡SAL DEL COCHE! ¡VENGA! ¡VENGA!
¡YO SOY EL UNITED STATES BORDER PATROL! ¡SAL
DEL COCHE! ¡SAL DEL COCHE CON LAS MANOS EN-
CIMA DE LA CABEZA! ¡AL SUELO! ¡AL SUELO!
¡VENGA! ¡CÁLLATE! Yeah. That's how we do it.
(Rest)
Nothing.
(Rest)
"Sometimes I turn a blind eye." No don't say that. But
it's true. A misstep. An indiscretion. Ramirez taking an
hour and 5 minutes for lunch. Flowers not filling out the
paperwork like he should. Carter getting a little too friendly
with some Tonk girl, and I know he's going to get intimate
with her when he's pulling the night shift solo. "Hide it
under the rug. Let the sleeping dog lie. Letting things slide
sometimes is necessary for the greater good. Of course,
strictly speaking, letting things slide is just the beginning of
the slippery slope. But what can you do. We're like a family,
us Patrol guys, out here." Yeah, say that. "Us against them.
Gotta do what I can to maintain that. I set the example.
I bend and flex up to a point. I make accommodations.
I don't overdo it, but I do what I can. Because, hey, we are
family, after all."

He continues scanning the horizon.

Chapter 51

Buddy and Grace still squaring off.

Grace

The Book of Grace, Chapter 51: The Luxury of Perspective.

Grace's notepad is visible from where she dropped it earlier.
She picks it up, tucking it in her pocket.
She turns on some music. Something upbeat.
She dances around.

Grace
Dance with me.

Buddy
I don't dance.

Grace
Your dad doesn't either.

Buddy
Whatever.

Grace
I touched a nerve.

Buddy
Buddy

Grace
I touched a nerve. I can tell. When I said "you're back to celebrate your dad!" I touched a nerve.

Buddy
It's all good.

Buddy
Buddy

Grace
How about some eggs? It's no trouble for me to burn some eggs.

She starts cooking eggs.

Grace
I wanted to have a party. Happy Homecoming! But when you didn't show yesterday Vet squashed it.

Buddy
Whatever.

Grace
The last time you were here. God. You were 10 years old. It was a horrible horrible day. Vet and your mom in here yelling. Yelling like they were trying to yell the house down. Both of them saying awful things. And you and me sat on the porch outside. And your shoelaces dragging.
(Rest)
You were 10. I was twice that. Twice that plus some.

Buddy
Yep.

Grace
(Rest)
I'm sorry your mom died. And about your house too.

(Rest)
You and me on the porch. Me and Vet were newly married. You were 10. I was worried about you. And you didn't want to tie your shoes. You didn't want to tie your shoes and you didn't want me to tie them for you. You just wanted them to drag around in the dirt.

Buddy
That's right.

Grace
You want some cake? It's not the first time somebody got cake and eggs. Most people get steak and eggs though. What do you say?
(Rest)
Buddy?

Buddy
It's hard being here. He hates me, I hate him.

Grace
He doesn't hate you. And you don't hate him. Not deep down. Not deep deep deep deep deep deep deep deep down you don't.
(Rest)
Deep deep

Grace	**Buddy**
Deep deep deep deep.	Deep deep deep deep.

A moment of levity.

Grace
When I saw you sleeping there, the first thing that came into my head was Camp David. You know, the place where the leaders of the world go to sort out their problems. I saw you sleeping there and I said to myself, I said, "Grace, Camp David begins at home."
(Rest)

"That's a stupid-dumb" idea, right? That's what Vet would say to that. You shoulda visited us over the years. We shoulda invited you. Better now than never, though. And whatever he says, he's giving it a go so I gotta hand it to him and here you are so I gotta hand it to you too.

> She hands him the eggs. He just holds the plate.

Grace
You should eat.

Buddy
I'm not hungry.

Buddy
Grace

Grace
"Camp David begins at home," I said to myself. And then I touched a nerve. But we can let that go, right? Put it behind us. Of course we can. Pretend like it never happened. Start fresh. Right? What do you say?

> He steals a kiss. A quick peck on the cheek.

Buddy
We made a baby just now.

Grace
You used to say that when you were small.

Buddy
Maybe it's true.

Grace
You're silly.

Buddy
Maybe we just did.

> He reaches for her. She moves out of his range.

Grace
You're really silly.

Buddy
Sorry.

Grace
Don't be sorry, just—don't—

Buddy
I touched a nerve.

Grace
—Not at all.
(Rest)

He starts eating.

Grace
You know what I think, Mr. Silly? I think you and Vet ought
to work together. Both of you, father and son, side by side,
working Border Patrol.

Buddy
It's not like I've got a job lined up anywhere else, so—

Grace
So you'll stay. And work with Vet. Now we just gotta mention
it to him. After he gets his medal he's going to be in a great
mood. I say we bring it up then.

Buddy
I already brought it up.

Grace
Oh. Ok. So, what'd he say?

Buddy
He said something about showing me around tonight.

Grace
He's taking you on a tour?

Buddy
I might not go.

Grace
You gotta go, Buddy. He took me on a tour. On our first date.
You gotta go. He's opening the door for you. And you'll do
your part and walk through it. If you two are going to make
up you can't expect him to do all the work.

Buddy
Kiss and make up.

Grace
You don't got to kiss him, silly. Shake his hand. Look him in
the eye. Stand up straight. Shoulders back. Show him that
you're—that you're wonderful.

Buddy
I'm not wonderful.

Grace
Sure you are.

Buddy
He wants me to get a haircut.

Grace
So get a haircut.

Buddy
We'll see.

Grace
You two are just alike.

Buddy
Is that a good thing?

Grace
Buddy

Grace
You'll get the job and before you know it, you'll be walking around in the uniform. And then you'll get your own place. You'll meet a nice girl. You two will have a couple of kids and you'll be living in your own house right down the street.

Buddy
And you won't send me any more letters.

Grace
Sure I will.

Buddy
Not if I'm right down the street.

Grace
Neighbors send letters all the time. Happy Birthday! Merry Christmas! Get Well Soon! And if you need it, I'll tuck some money inside like I used to.
(Rest)
I guess that little bit of money I was sending you and your mom didn't amount to squat. We would of sent more but things are tight.

Buddy
Those stories you sent were better than the money.

Grace
They were just newspaper clippings.

Buddy
They were nice.

Grace
At the diner, when I bus the tables I save the paper. Most people just leave it behind. At first I was trying to be, you know, "green." You know, thinking I'd recycle it. I had a

whole big stack of newspapers from saving them. Then I had
some—some time on my hands. And I started reading them.
Clipping out things.

Buddy
I liked the story about the dog.

Grace
I thought you would.

Buddy
A dog named Trouble. And the Disney World one.

Grace
Disney*land*. I get them mixed up too. I haven't been to
either one of them. Disneyland's the one with the original
Magic Castle. The second one's like, a copy.

Buddy
Right. I like how it said when she saw that castle as a kid
and it looked so big and then, how she went back when she
was all grown up, and how it looked so small. How she could
feel the whole passage of time right in that very moment.
What'd she call it?

Grace
The "luxury of perspective."

Buddy
Right. I used to think this house was huge.

Grace
Maybe cause of all the land around it. All the land we've
got around it. And you were little. When you're little even a
small house looks big.

Buddy
Some things don't get smaller, though. Some things get bigger. Worse.

Grace

And some things get better. "Look on the bright side for crying out loud it don't cost hardly nothing." That's what I tell Vet. More cake?

Buddy

No thanks. Mom was sick. She got sicker. Bills for the house got bigger. And I was just—lost. Then I saw him on the tv. Out of the fucking blue. And as mad as I was at him, all I wanted was to get here, and sit with you on the porch. Cause as bad as it was, last time I was here, somehow you made it ok. You made it—nice.

Grace

Thanks.

Buddy

Too hot to sit outside now.

Grace

Yeah.

Buddy

You were sitting near me when I was sleeping. Doing what? Watching me?

Grace

Just sitting.

Buddy

You were writing.

Grace

Grocery list.

Buddy

Right.
(Rest)
"We the people . . . in order to form a more perfect union, establish justice, ensure domestic tranquility, provide for the

common defense, promote the general welfare and secure the blessings of liberty to ourselves and our posterity do ordain and establish this Constitution."
(Rest)
I got it all memorized, pretty much.

Grace
Let's hear the rest.

Buddy
Point is, we're establishing our Constitution. We're going to be friends, right?

Grace
Better than friends. We're family. By law anyway.

Buddy
So tell me something about you. A secret. I feel like you know a lot about me and I don't know anything about you. Go on. I won't tell.

Grace
You first. Go.

Buddy
I used to be scared of Vet. When I was a kid. Maybe I still am. Secret.

Grace
I took a class once. I kept it secret from Vet. Algebra.

Buddy
Algebra. Whoa. Algebra! So you can solve for X and stuff?

Grace
Yes.

Buddy
You pass?

Grace

A couple of As on a couple of tests. Then Vet found out. He didn't like me going.
(Rest)
The teacher, he really liked me. Not in that way, but still, I had to quit.
(Rest)
Secret.

Buddy

I don't have anymore.

Grace

Yeah you do. Go.

Buddy

You go.

Grace

You go. Secret.

Buddy

That hole in the yard. He dug it for you, right?

Grace

He says it's a "deterrent."

Buddy

He dug one for my mom.

Grace

But he never used it.

Buddy

No, he never used it. It just sat there. Where she could see it. Every day.
(Rest)
He used to hit my mom. He hit you?

Grace
Buddy

Buddy
Yes, right?

Grace
Grace

Buddy holds up two fingers. It's Strike Two.

Grace
Peace?

Buddy
We'll see. Maybe. "Peace out." Maybe.

Grace
Here's one you'll never guess. I'm writing a book.

Buddy
That's what you were doing.

Grace
Collecting my thoughts, yeah.

Buddy
And then writing them down.

Grace
And then rounding them up.

Buddy
Show me.

She goes to the rug, pushing it aside. She removes
a few pieces of loose flooring,
pulling out several scribbled-on waitress pads,
a few stray newspaper articles and, then,
her red-marbled composition book, her *Book of Grace*.

Buddy
What's it called?

Grace
The Book of Grace.

Buddy
Named her after yourself. What's it about?

Grace
Kind of like—I dunno—the evidence of good things.

Buddy
The evidence of good things.

Grace
Yeah.
(Rest)
When I see a newspaper story that's nice, I cut it out and
paste it in. The clippings I sent to you I copied down in here
so we could both have them. I got a picture of the president
in here somewhere. But it's not just clippings, sometimes,
at the diner, someone'll tell me a story and I'll write it down,
or sometimes I see something interesting and write it down.
Some stuff I just make up. My thoughts. About—about
things. I started it after I had to quit that math class.
It's kind of like a self-help book.

Buddy
I bet it'll be a bestseller.

Grace
I dunno about all that, but, sometimes I pretend it's published.
Dumb, right?

Buddy
No

Grace
Sometimes, you know, when those writers read, like at the
library? Sometimes, when I read it out loud to myself, I set
up chairs in here and pretend.
(Rest)
Stupid, right?

Buddy
No.

> Playfully, Buddy snatches her Book, leafing through it.

Grace
Hey—

Buddy
It's beautiful. You can draw too.

Grace
Yeah. Gimmie.

> Buddy, reading from her Book:

Buddy
"I like snakes. All kinds. Something deep within my nature, I guess . . . Most people don't like snakes, and so, I guess, me liking snakes sets me apart from most people."

Grace
Give it back.

> Instead of handing it over, he holds the Book close to his chest.

Buddy
"The evidence of good things." How's it end?

Grace
I'm not there yet.
(Rest)
"Stupid-dumb!" That's what Vet would say if he knew I was writing a book.
(Rest)
Gimmie.

> But he continues to hold the Book close.

Buddy
Buddy

Buddy
Snake
Snake
Buddy

Snake
Snake

(Rest)

Snake
I just changed my name. Just right now. To Snake.

Grace
Snake.

Snake
Yeah. It suits me better than "Buddy." It's cool, right?

Grace
It might be.

Snake
You like snakes. And it suits me. "Evidence of good things!"
You'll see.

Grace
Footnote #3:

> We see Vet on the job. He pauses from his patrol work.

Vet
My nickname used to be "Snake." Back in the day. But I'm
on the good foot now.

Snake
Pop, he used to go by Snake.

Grace
Yeah, I know.

Snake
You think I'm following in his footsteps?

Grace
For you to know and for me to find out. Good thing I like snakes.

Snake
Yeah. It's a good thing. Secret.

Grace
Your dad's really glad you're here.

Snake
That's a secret even from him.

Grace
He's glad. You'll see.
(Rest)
Secret.

Snake
What if I'm on the bad foot?

Grace
What if that's just your mad-self talking?

Snake
If I was bad, could you turn me into something good?

Grace
Footnote #4:

Again, Vet pauses from work.

Vet
And did I ever tell you about the time he put a firecracker in
my car? That thing went bang and I just about wet myself.
I'm laughing but it wasn't funny. That kid is bad news.
Bad through and through.

Grace
When you were little, sitting on the porch, you kept saying
"I'm a bad boy. I'm a bad boy." I can see why you'd think
that. But you were never really bad.

Snake
What if I was? What if I am?

Grace
You're still that ten-year-old kid with his untied shoes trying
to impress me.

Snake
And you're still good gracious Grace trying to make
everything turn out all right.

Grace
Snake

Snake
I'll go get that haircut.

> Using his phone, he takes their selfie.

Grace
And you'll let Vet show you around?

Snake
Looking on the bright side don't cost nothing.

Grace
There you go.

> He starts to leave.

Grace
Snake. My Book.

> Snake hands her back her Book. He goes on his way,
> leaving Grace to her work.

Chapter 52

> Grace works, copying her notes into her red Book.

Grace
Chapter 52: *The Book of Grace.*

> Day turns into evening. Evening turns into night.
> She takes a break from working, setting up chairs
> and reading from her Book to her imaginary audience.

Grace
Good evening. I'm going to read a little bit from *The Book of Grace*. It's a work-in-progress. Today, just for fun, I'm gonna start from my latest entry and then I'll read backwards all the way to the beginning. And we'll see what that's like. Ok. Here's something from today:
(Rest)
A friend of mine came home today. Not "home" but to his father's house. Which, in this case, isn't the same thing. He also took his father's name today. Snake. Funny how you can take someone's name. Junior when you're born. I took, when I got married, I took my husband's name: Smith. My husband's nickname used to be Snake. That would make him Snake

Smith. He's on the good foot now. And his son, now Snake
Smith Junior, he's following in his father's footsteps. So he
must be heading towards being on the good foot too. Except
that snakes don't have feet. Well.
(Rest)
My husband's son, he's all grown up. But he's still just as silly
as he can be.
(Rest)
He changed his name because of something he read in my
book. Maybe this book is worth something after all.

> She looks through her previously written pages,
> looking for something in particular.
> Finding it.

Grace
Evidence of Good Things: The Magic Castle. Here it is.

> She shows us, then finds another interesting page.

Grace
More evidence of good: from Chapter 44: It snowed today. In
the middle of summer. It was like a miracle.
(Rest)
Ok. From Chapter 43: More Evidence of Good: That baby
who was stolen from the hospital got reunited with her loving
parents 23 years later. There's a pig in China born without
any back legs and the farmer didn't slaughter it, instead he
keeps it as a pet and it hops around on its front legs and gets
along just fine. And that lady, she got shot in the head. But
she didn't die.*
(Rest)
From Chapter 40: More Evidence of Good:
(Rest)
Will, the cowboy, came in the diner today wanting grits and
we were out of grits and he was about to pitch a fit and then
he started laughing instead and we all laughed and he had
white toast instead of grits.

*Use these 3 stories or the production may insert their own 3 pieces of
Evidence.

(Rest)

From Chapter 39: Today I got word from Buddy. He says he's coming to his father's Ceremony. How about that? Today I'm feeling like everything broken can mend. Today I'm feeling like a Gold Star.

(Rest)

From Chapter 37: Charlotte's daughter Charlotte plays the tuba. She's in the marching band. The tuba is bigger than she is. She came in today and played her part of "Deep in the Heart of Texas." It didn't sound like much cause it was just the tuba part: bom-bom-bom-bom. But I clapped really hard when she was done cause it's important to encourage people. Especially when they're young. So they can get in the habit of hearing it.

(Rest)

From Chapter 30: Today I was looking in the icebox for frozen broccoli and instead I found some old Halloween candy! How about that?

Mine

(Rest)

From Chapter 23: Today I put my foot down and insisted that we invite Buddy to our house because he hasn't been here for many years.

(Rest)

I wonder if forgiveness is possible? I think so. I hope so.

(Rest)

What if we outsource forgiveness. Heck, we're outsourcing everything else. Then your forgiveness would come with a sticker that says "made in India" or "made in China" or "made in Farawayville."

(Rest)

That makes me think of plastic bags. They say there's a big stretch of trash in the middle of the ocean. Like a land mass, but it's really just a gob of trash. It's practically the size of Texas, that's how big they say it is. I use plastic bags. Do you? But it's not like I throw my bags into the ocean.

> She hears the sound of a car. She scrambles to hide her Book.
> Then the sound turns to silence and the coast is clear.
> She goes back to reading.

Grace

From Chapter 19:

(Rest)

Today I am thinking about the Rut. It's like, sometimes your life is a Rut, a Rut you've dug yourself. Sometimes your life-groove can become a Rut. Sometimes someone you're with, say your husband, or your wife, or your town, or your job, sometimes your repeated day-to-day can make a Rut or sometimes your S.O., aka, your Significant Other, sometimes they dig a Rut for you to live in and you don't notice cause the Rut looks like a groove, a thing with promise, but it's not a groove at all, it's a Rut. And by walking the Rut, by living in it, you only make it deeper.

(Rest)

Where do I begin? Where does "me" start? What is the past tense of "Us"? "Used." The past tense of "Us" is "Used." As in my "used-to-be."

(Rest)

That sounds stupid. Needs work. Stupid-dumb. S-h-i-t.

(Rest)

Sometimes I spell out bad words. Cause I read somewhere that we each have, inside of us, an "inner child." And I don't want mine hearing me say bad language. It's silly, but I think it improves me. Are there things you'd like to try that might improve you?

(Rest)

More Evidence of Good: Javier, our busboy is learning Japanese. When I ask him how come Japanese he just smiles.

(Rest)

From Chapter 10: My friend, Cowboy Will, he's got this story about a dog. A dog he had years ago. When he was a much younger man. That dog was pure trouble. And that was its name too: Trouble. How was that dog ever gonna do anything good with a name like that? One day Will gets so tired of the dog he puts him in his truck and drives 100 miles away and dumps him on the side of the road. End of story? No. Will says there's an end to it, but he won't tell me. He will not for the life of him tell me how that story ends. So I've made up some endings for myself:

(Rest)

I say there's a flash flood and a drowning man, and Trouble jumps in the river and saves the man and the man renames him Savior.

(Rest)

Or I say Trouble's just walking along and some kids are going to the circus and he follows them and joins the circus and travels the world.

(Rest)

Maybe you could make up your own ending to that story. Try it. It's fun.

(Rest)

(Rest)

This is Trouble.

She shows a picture of the dog.

Grace

Also mine

From Chapter 6: More Basic Guidelines: Know your cowboys. For example: it has occurred to me that there are two kinds of cowboys: a cowboy with a horse and a cowboy without a horse. A cowboy with a horse is a real cowboy. A cowboy without a horse is just a guy that wears the clothes. Which one are you?

(Rest)

Everything reminds you of something, after a while. Like when you move to a new town and nothing is familiar and then, after a few years, you look around and hear yourself saying to yourself: Here is where I met him, over there is the last time I saw her, that's the place where I stood with the chocolate double-dip cone and felt happy, there is where the bad thing happened, and there's the lake where we all jumped in.

(Rest)

More Basic Guidelines: You can either spread the love or spread the shit. Your choice.

(Rest)

From Chapter 3: Today, walking home from work, I saw a snake. And that got me to thinking. I like snakes. All kinds. Something deep within my nature, I guess . . . Me liking snakes sets me apart from most people. What do you like that sets you apart?

(Rest)

From Chapter 2: On Hope: It's good to hope. Hopes can be large or small. One of my hopes involves a piece of clothing, specifically, a dress. It's very pretty. It's red. It's been hanging in the window of our local department store for a long time now. You could say I've put my name on it, even though I don't dare buy it. Still, it's mine.

(Rest)

From Chapter 1:

(Rest)

I like algebra and some day I would like to live in The House of Wisdom.

(Rest)

Did you know that "The ancient science of algebra was invented by the revered Persian, Muhammad ibn Musa al-Khwarizmi. He wrote a book called *Algebra*. He was perhaps an orthodox Muslim. He was born around 780 and, in addition to being considered the father of algebra, he was also an accomplished astronomer, astrologer and geographer. He lived for many years in Baghdad, living and working in a place called The House of Wisdom."

(Rest)

Here's more from Chapter 1, my first entry:

Today Vet got mad at me and he dug a hole in the yard. And he told me I had to quit my math class so I quit it. And when he went to work, I started this book. I'm calling it *The Book of Grace*.

(Rest)

(Rest)

That's all. Thank you.

> Smiling to herself, she might take a little bow
> to her imaginary audience. Then she turns on the radio,
> resets the living room chairs and
> puts away her Book as the lights fade.
> Intermission.

Chapter 53

Much later. In the wee hours.

Grace
The Book of Grace, Chapter 53: It's Bigger Than I Thought.

Grace retires to the bedroom.
The guys come home.
Snake, with his fresh haircut,
watching new video-playback on his phone.
Vet following behind.

Vet
You're quiet.

Snake
I'm thinking about it.

Vet
Thumbs up or thumbs down. Does my speech work? Say something.

Snake
Gimmie a minute.

Vet

I showed you the Fence. I extended you a privilege. I'm not some goddamn tour guide, but there I was, acting like some goddamn tour guide, telling you the history of it.

Snake

I'm taking it all in.

Vet

You were taking pictures.

Snake

Video. Like you got. I liked it.

Vet

You liked it?

Snake

The Fence. Yeah.

Vet

Anything else?

Snake

It's bigger than I thought.

Vet

Anything else?

Snake

You've got the one in China beat.

Vet

We beat China? How so.

Snake

Yours is active.

Vet

Damn right.

Snake

You beat Berlin cause yours is still standing. And you got the one in the Middle East beat cause yours is longer.

Vet

Pretty much.

Snake

See, I'm thinking about the Fence.

Vet

You—you thinking about anything else?

Snake

The Fence, it's kind of filling up my whole mind, you know?

Vet

It grows on you.

Snake

Maybe I could work there.

Vet

Let's wait on that.

Snake

Hurry up and wait.

Vet

Don't get ahead of yourself, that's all.

Snake

But, it could happen. The guys seemed to like me. I fit socially. That's no small thing. Not everybody does, right?

Vet

Right.

Snake fiddles with his phone, looking at his footage.

Snake

Mind if I share this footage with my friends?

Vet

You've got friends?

Snake

I'm part of an online community.

Vet

You didn't video anything that's classified, so go ahead.
Sure.

Snake

Gr8.

Vet

Goddamnit to hell, aren't you going to say anything about my
speech?!

Snake

Like what?

Vet

Like anything.

Snake

It's real interesting.

Vet

"Real interesting"? You're smug cause you took some
college classes.

Snake

I'm not smug.

Vet

You've got the Constitution and the Declaration all
memorized and you stood there spouting it off for the guys
and what did I do? Did I tell you to shut up?

Snake
You let me talk.

Vet
Damn right I let you talk. On and on and on. And I even led in the goddamned applause.

Snake
Ramirez clapped first.

Vet
But I joined in, didn't I? And I whistled hooray. I even complimented your haircut. You're a show-off. You're a goddamned show-off!

Snake
I'm out of here.

> Snake gets his footlocker. Starts to go.

Vet
You're staying. What's it going to look like with you showing up and then leaving? They'd have a good time with that, I'm telling you. You're staying. You're staying.

> Grace comes out of the bedroom, wearing her bathrobe and slip.

Grace
How'd it go?

Vet
Complete waste of time.

Snake
I liked the Fence.

Vet
I need some sleep.

Snake
And I liked your speech too, ok?

Vet
You liked my speech?

Grace
You did your speech for him?

Vet
In the truck. On the way home.

Grace
You haven't done it for me. Say it again.

Vet
It's still pretty rough.

Snake
I liked it.
(Rest)
I got some pointers, though. If you're interested.

Grace
Vet
Snake
Grace

Grace
I'll go back to bed.

> She gives Vet a kiss and goes back into the bedroom.

Snake
You should say it out loud for Grace. See what she thinks.

Vet
Thinks? Jesus. She thinks I should open up. She wants me
to go bleeding all over them.

Snake
I'm thinking a 180 on that.

Vet

Me too.

Snake

You need to give them something they can fix their minds
to. Everything in your speech should be substantial. Like
the meat and potatoes that they'll be chewing on, something
that they'll be talking about long after you're done talking.
Not rambling. Not vague. Not poetic. Not personal.
Not revealing. Something solid and commanding.

Vet

Something that'll stick in their minds long after I'm done
running my mouth.

Snake

Exactly. So that, when they look at you from here on out,
they'll be thinking of the words you said to them. You'll
be just doing your day-to-day and they'll be running your
words in their heads. And they'll stand a little straighter in
your presence. Your words'll be like the Fence itself.

Vet

Right.

Snake

And don't start off with "Aliens."

Vet

It was just an idea.

Snake

Don't have "Aliens" anywhere in it.

Vet

Right.

Snake

Makes you sound like a—a nut job.
(Rest)
Run it one more time and let's see.

Vet

Not right now. I need to keep my own counsel with it. Maybe later.

Snake

You'll be up there talking before you know it.

Vet

Maybe later I said.

Snake

Suit yourself.

Vet

You think you're Border Patrol material?

Snake

Sure.

Vet

But it's not about what you think, is it?

Snake

I guess not.

Vet

Let's see what you've got.

>   Vet drops to the floor and starts doing push-ups.
>   When Snake joins him, Vet stands and talks.

Vet

Three Tonks armed to the teeth. You've been tracking them for days. Suddenly you find them. What do you do?

Grace

Footnote #5:

>   Grace, from the bedroom, eavesdropping, answering for herself.

Vet

What would you do?

Grace

((I would call for back up.))

Snake

Call for back up, right?

Vet

Back up is a long time coming.

> Now, jumping jacks.

Snake

I would go in with guns blazing. Figuring my firepower will beat theirs.

Vet

Or theirs would beat yours.

Snake

So I'd—die in the line of duty. Defending our Border. That'd be good, right? Right?

Vet

That's "brave."

Snake

Brave is good, right?

> Now, running in place.

Vet

You're on Patrol and you catch up with another one. This time, this one's really nice. Sneaked in all alone. Speaks good English. A sort of poetic soul. Read the stars to find his way north. All he wants is a better life for himself. He'll get an honest job and send his earnings back home. He's a good guy. But a Tonk. He's got a bag of money for you if you'd look the other way. What do you do?

Grace
Footnote #6: ((I would take the money and let him slip in.))

Snake
I wouldn't take the money.

Vet
Pesos or greenbacks?

> Now, full up-down squats.

Grace
((Pesos or greenbacks?))

Snake
Money is money is money. What difference does it make?

Vet
Does he have pesos or greenbacks? Ask.

Grace
((Does he have pesos or greenbacks?))

Snake
Does he have pesos or greenbacks? Cause greenbacks'd be worth more.

Vet
Bingo. Let's say he's got a big bag of greenbacks.

Snake
So I would *want* to take the money, but I *don't* take the money. Right?

Grace
((Right.))

> Vet switches to sit-ups. Snake follows suit.
> This time Vet keeps talking as he drills.

Vet

Say he tries to strike a bargain. The greenbacks in exchange for him to be allowed to just sneak back home.

Snake

No way, José. I'd turn him in.

Vet

And all those greenbacks he had would probably "disappear."

Snake

Sometimes that happens.

> Vet finishes his sit-ups.
> Snake continues with his.

Vet

Oh, does it?

Snake

Yeah. But it wouldn't happen with me. Not on my watch!

Grace

(((Gold Star, Buddy.))

> The pop quiz has concluded. Grace goes back to bed.

Snake

(Rest)

How am I doing? Did I pass?

> Vet walks to the refrigerator. Snake finishes his sit-ups and stands.

Snake

Did I pass?

> Vet, holding a beer, walks over to the rug.
> Pretending it's just an accident, he toes back the rug.
> Snake replaces the rug. Vet notices that.

Snake

Did I pass, yes or no?

Vet
I'll let you know, Buddy.

Snake
Snake.

Vet
Right. Snake. Have a seat.

> Vet sits on the couch. Snake tentatively joins him.

Vet
Unwind. We're just home from work. We've got a big day tomorrow. Now we unwind.

Snake
Right.

> Vet's relaxed. Drinking. Snake is tense.

Vet
You nervous?

Snake
Not at all.

Vet
I like to unwind with entertainment.

Snake
Watching the Fence?

Vet
Better.

Snake
Like what.

> Vet goes to his footlocker.

Vet
I got hot stuff in here.

> Vet unlocks his locker, showing piles of videotapes.

Vet
Your pick.

Snake
What's on them?

Vet
Girls.

Snake
Girls?

Vet
Girls. Your pick.

Snake
The cases all look the same, no pictures or nothing. No names.

Vet
More exciting that way. Like a game of chance. Pick.

> Snake chooses a tape. Vet puts it in the player, retakes his seat.

Snake
You should upgrade your technology.

Vet
The picture's fine. Pretty girls, right?

Snake
Yeah.

> The girlie-porn video plays on the tv and the light plays on
> their faces. The sound is barely audible.
> Parts of the video are reflected on a window or a wall.

Vet

I like to just kinda sit here and let them do their thing.
Kinda like background music. Kinda like ambiance. It
unwinds my mind.

Snake

Right.

> The 2 men sit there watching porn. They look like
> they're watching paint dry.

Vet

The Ceremony's going to be something. I'll stand at the
Fence and give my speech. Standing there getting my medal.
Icing on the gravy.
(Rest)
You telling them how you're "Snake" and how I used to be
"Snake." That went over all right.

Snake

Yeah, it did. They looked at you with respect.

Vet

Yeah. They did.
(Rest)
Your mother didn't want to have anything to do with you.
Came here trying to dump you on me. But I couldn't take
you in. You were—troubled. And I was starting fresh. It
wouldn't of been fair to Grace. You were like a whole can
of worms and I was making a fresh start.

Snake

Is that an apology?

Vet

No. I'm just telling you what was going on.
(Rest)
Maybe I could get you some help. Somebody to go talk to,
you know, once a week like they do.

Snake

No thanks.

(Rest)

Let's hear it again. Your speech.

Vet

I'm working it out in my head. When I stand up there saying it, you'll hear it fresh.

Snake

Have you written it out?

Vet

I've composed it. But I wouldn't write it down.

Snake

You should totally write a book. *Veteran of the Border Patrol.* That would really put you out in front.

Vet

Only I don't think much of books. Books cause a weakening of the mind. You write something down you don't use your brain muscles to remember it. Take, for example, your Cro-Magnon man. Or your Neanderthal. Or your Australopithecus. He may have had a smaller brain than we do today, but he used it to the fullest. He had to remember where the game was and how to get home after he'd bagged it. And he didn't have a GPS. He didn't have advanced technology. Plus, when things are in your head, they're safe. Less chance of theft.

> He looks at Snake's footlocker.

Vet

For the job, there'll be a thorough background check. They'll look through all your personals.

> He examines his ring of keys, selecting one. Trying it. No luck.
> He tries another. He unlocks Snake's footlocker
> and is about to raise the lid before Snake stops him.

Snake
You already searched it once. What are you scared of?

Vet
Snake

(Rest)

Vet backs off.

Vet
I'll be up there with the governor. I'll be getting my medal.

Snake
And I'll be wearing mine.

Vet
You'll wear yours.

Snake
Sure.

Vet
You should just wear the bar pin. You don't want to be too loud with it.

Snake
I lost that part so I'll have to wear the whole medal. Right on my lapel. It's not regulation but it'll be all right.

Vet
You'll want everybody to see it.

Snake
Sure. Why not.

Vet
You'll want to show it off.

Snake
I earned it. It's mine.

Vet
You wanna steal my thunder.

Snake
Oh, come on, Pop.

Vet
Too bad you can't get on the job in time for the governor's visit, right? Is that what you're thinking?

Snake
I'm ok to meet him as just a civilian.

Vet
And flash your medal.

Snake
Sure. Plus, being your son.

Vet
Following in my footsteps.

Snake
That's right.

Vet
Legacy.

Snake
Yeah. That'll be something, right? Us both working Border Patrol. Side by side. I got the job, don't I? It's a go, right?

Vet
It's a no. It wouldn't work. You wouldn't work. Not around me.

Snake
You gotta give me a hand. I'm good enough, right? I'm good enough. It's normal to give your kid a hand, Pop.

Vet
You'll find your feet. Just not here. Somewhere else.

Snake
Come on, Pop.

Vet
You'll find your feet. Just not with me, just not in my footsteps. It'll be better that way. For both of us.

Snake
Vet
Snake

> It's Strike Three. Snake flashes three fingers. Gently, defeated.

Snake
Three.

Vet
Three what?

Snake
The three of us here. You, me and Grace. That's three.

Vet
You understand about the job, right? There's plenty of jobs in the universe. You'll find one somewhere out there just not here, ok?

Snake
Sure. Ok.

> Vet glances at the clock. Drinks. Snake watches the tv.
> Time passes. Vet eventually falls asleep on the couch.
> Snake gets up, puts away the porn video, turns on the live feed and,
> alone, watches the Fence. After a beat, he fiddles with his phone.
> Grace comes out of the bedroom.
> Men on couch. Vet sleeping. Snake texting. Fence video going.

Grace
Hey.

Snake
Hey.

> She lovingly helps Vet up, helping him to bed.
> Then, coming out of the bedroom, she gets her Book
> from its hiding place under the floor.

Grace
Talking with your friends?

Snake
Texting.

Grace
In a chatroom?

Snake
Yeah.

Grace
Nice haircut.

Snake
Thanks.

> She goes outside, sits on the porch, reading from her Book.
> Snake comes outside to watch her.

Snake
It's not working out.

Grace
I heard. When things are bad I read this and it helps me feel better.

Snake
It's not getting any better with him.

Grace
Not right now, but it will. Plenty of bad things turn good in the fullness of time.

Snake
Sometimes bad things go from bad to worse.

Grace
Not always.
(Rest)
It's bigger than I thought, the stuff between you two, right?

Snake
Yeah.
(Rest)
The things he did to me. When we were all living together.
Me and him and Mom.

Grace
Like what?

> Vet, in the bedroom, sits on the bed. Awake but not listening.

Snake
Unspeakable. Saying it was my fault, saying I was the bad
one. And that he was just trying to keep me in line. That's
what he had to do, you know? Keep the bad one in line.
(Rest)
I just went from bad to worse.

Grace
But you were never bad.

Snake
I'm going to blow something up.
(Rest)
I'm going to blow something up. You heard me.

Grace
That's just your mad-self talking.
(Rest)
Buddy?

Snake
Snake.
(Rest)
Can I read it?

Grace
Ok.

> Snake takes her Book, choosing pages at random,
> reading to himself. Then aloud.

Snake
Disneyland.
(Rest)
The dog named Trouble.
(Rest)
The House of Wisdom.

Grace
No one's ever read it but you.
(Rest)
What?

Snake
Nothing.

> More pages read silently to himself. Then aloud.

Snake
"Red dress."

Grace
Yeah. What?

Snake
Nothing.
(Rest)

> He closes the Book. Hands it back to her.

Grace
Did it help?

Snake
Nope.

Grace
You can read more—

Snake
No thanks.

Grace
Maybe it takes time. To sink in. Here I am, little Miss-
Wanna-Fix-It-All. Well, more like Mrs.-Wanna-Fix-It-All now.

Snake
Leave me alone, all right?

Grace
All right. Sure.

> She scoots a distance away from him,
> then gets up, about to go.

Snake
You ever thought of leaving him?

Grace
Yeah. But your troubles follow you.

Snake
Not if you do something about it.

Grace
Maybe I should change my name.

Snake
Don't. Grace suits you.

Grace
Snake

(Rest)

> With Book in hand she goes inside,
> putting it away, then heading to bed.

Snake on the porch alone.
He takes out his phone. Starts making a selfie-video.

Snake
The Book of Snake, Chapter One: "We hold these truths to be self-evident, that all men—" No—
(Rest)
The Book of Snake, Chapter One.
(Rest)
"When in the course of human events it becomes necessary for a people—"
(Rest)
For a people to what?
(Rest)
Hhhhhhh.

He quits his selfie. Just sitting on the porch
as the wee hours change to dawn.
Then he exits.

Chapter 54

Grace
Chapter 54: *The Book of Snake.*

> Morning. Vet, ready for work, prepares his dress uniform for later.
> Grace, ready for work, comes from the kitchen with coffee.

Grace
I made coffee.

Vet
Where's the kid?

Grace
Gone for a walk, I guess.
(Rest)
That gives us some time—

> She hugs him romantically. He pulls away.

Vet
Don't. I've gotta go down there, make sure things are set up, and then come back here and get dressed. I can't be late today, huh? Hurry up if you want a ride in.

Grace

I'll leave the door open for him.

Vet

Don't worry about him. Come on.

Grace exits. Hours pass.

Around noon, Snake enters, whistling a tune.

He carries a nice shopping bag from his recent expedition.

After making sure the coast is clear, he deposits the bag's

contents in the bedroom. He returns to the living room.

Taking his phone out of his pocket,

he records himself as he speaks.

Snake

The Book of Snake, Chapter One.

He stops recording. Deletes. Starts over.

Snake

The Book of Snake, Chapter One.
(Rest)
The Book of Snake, as told to you by Snake himself, coming
to you recorded from—from the grounds of my training
compound. And to be broadcast throughout the world in the
fullness of time. Ok.
(Rest)
Three Strikes. He's got Three Strikes against him. Three
Strikes and now he's out.
(Rest)
You're probably at a similar place in your life. That's why
you're watching this. You're probably watching this and
wondering what to do. Like me you've done good, or if not
all good, then you've done as good as you could. As good
as you could within the confines of his rules. Living, if you
want to call it that, bowing, stooping, scraping, crawling,
working, just to get by, just to make ends meet. Punching his
clock. On his time. We gave him a chance, didn't we? We've

been trying to work within his rules, haven't we? More or less, right? More or less.

(Rest)

Trying to work within some rules made by a man. Made by, made by *"The* Man." His clock. His rules. His order of things. His system. And guess what: his system don't work for us.

(Rest)

Evidence of good: None. Evidence of bad: Strike One. Strike One is a crime in his past. A crime that he will not even admit to. An unspeakable series of crimes made against our person. We have given him every opportunity to admit his crimes, but he has chosen to ignore said opportunities. And so he has earned Strike One.

(Rest)

Evidence of bad: Strike Two. Strike Two happened in the past and continues happening in the present. Strike Two involves both the past and current female members of the family unit which he beat down in the past and now, even with this fairly new member, continues the beating down and doesn't see anything wrong with it. So Strike Two.

(Rest)

The Man, he likes to promise you something better. I'm telling you you're a fool for wanting his better. Take his better like a trained dog, take his hand, take his handshake, live your life in the palm of his hand, and for what? So that when he makes a fist he can just crush you?

(Rest)

His systems and his rules and his laws, they aren't for you. They're for him. And the day has come for us to start wiping them out.

(Rest)

More evidence of bad things: Strike Three. He's not content to beat down your past, he's not content with beating down your present, that's right, he wants to beat down your future too, doesn't he? The Man was promising us something better, right? He was promising us some golden castle where we could, where we could eat ice cream every day, or whatever. You know what I'm talking about. You've heard his promises. All about what he's going to do for you. But he never does anything. He's got a carrot on a stick and he's just holding it out there in front of your face, just holding it out there, just holding it out there, he's a big man, promising you stuff, but one day you get it: he's not holding it out there for you, he's just holding out. And he's always going to be holding out on you. He doesn't got anything for you. He doesn't want you to succeed. He wants you to fail. And fail big. He wants to spin your good into bad. He wants to leave you with nothing, all broken and sad. He wants you to follow in his footsteps so he can feel big, but in the end, I'm telling you, he wants you jobless, homeless and hopeless; rejected, neglected and disrespected. You know what I'm talking about. So Strike Three.

> He opens his footlocker, taking out a hand grenade.

Snake

Maybe you, like me, Served. Maybe you like me had a mother and a house. Maybe you lost it all. And when you cried out to The Man he turned a blind eye and a deaf ear. Blind and deaf to you. Not wanting to have shit to do with you. Figuring we'll just dry up and blow away. Come again another day. Go away and come back tomorrow. Well tomorrow is now. And we are not going to blow away. Instead, we are going to blow him away.

> He hears Grace coming home. Quickly locking up his trunk,
> he takes his phone and grenade,
> heading through the backdoor and into the backyard.
> Grace, on the porch, looking through her most recent notes.
> Choosing what she'd like to add to her Book.

Snake

The Man likes keeping Us down. The Man has dug a hole for you, a hole in your yard with your name on it, and it's up to you to do something about that. Take some kind of action. He had his chances but he struck out. Strike One, Strike Two, Strike Three. 3-2-1-Boom.

> Entering the house, Grace checks to see that the coast is clear.
> She takes out her Book and transfers notes from her waitress pad.

In the backyard, Snake is holding his grenade
up to his phone. He continues recording.

Snake

Now we will strike. And when we strike against The Man, striking him at his Ceremony, we will be careful, we will be smart. And after we've struck him, and after we've wiped him out, we will escape. We will move on. To the next target. He's just the first of many. He's got it coming to him. He's got it coming. The push-back starts here. We gotta rise up. And I'm gonna lead the way. Snake. Snake. Snake will rise up and lead "We the people." Do not tread on me. Cause I will take you down.

(Rest)

(Rest)

The Book of Snake will continue. More later. Stay tuned.

Chapter X

> From inside the house Grace sees Snake
> in the distant backyard. Waves to him.
> He waves back.
> She works on her Book.

Grace
The Book of Grace, Chapter X: The House of Wisdom.

> Snake comes in carrying his phone and his hidden grenade.
> He goes to his footlocker,
> replacing the grenade without Grace noticing.

Grace
Vet's over there making sure everything's set up right. He'll be home soon, then we'll have to go, ok?

Snake
You're going?

Grace
Sure I'm going.

Snake
What if you don't?

Grace
I'm looking forward to it. It'll be fun.

Snake
But what if you don't go.

Grace
If I don't go I'll never hear the end of it. And if you don't go
I'll never hear the end of it. So we're going. I'll bet money
that, once he gets his medal, he'll change up about you
working with him. You'll see.

Snake
I don't want to work with him.

Grace
It's a good job.

Snake
I don't want a good job.

Grace
Sure you do.
(Rest)
We should start getting ready. If you need to use the shower
you should get in there now.

> Instead of heading to the shower, Snake goes to the radio,
> turning it on loud, enjoying the music.

Snake
Dance with me.

Grace
I gotta finish this.

Snake
Lots of "evidence of good things" today?

Grace
People from out of town visiting for the Ceremony, they were packing the diner. They had some good stories.

Snake
We never had my party. Come dance.

Grace
You're happy.

Snake
Yep.

Grace
What about?

Snake
Secret.

> He goes to the fridge. Takes out two beers. Opens both, handing one to Grace, drinking his down as she watches.

Grace
Tell me.

Snake
Not yet.
(Rest)
Cheers.

> He drinks. She doesn't. He gets another beer, opens it. Drinks.

Grace
Music's a little loud.

Snake
Sorry.

> He turns the radio down some. Keeps dancing.
> Shoots a selfie-video, including Grace in the shot.

Grace
You're making a movie.

Snake
It's a book.

Grace
Ok. Outside you were talking it out. I saw you. That's great. Good for you.

Snake
Cheers.

> They toast and drink.

Grace
What's your book about?

Snake
Secret.
(Rest)
I got something for you.

Grace
Tell me about your book.

Snake
It's hanging in your closet. Go look.
(Rest)
It's a present. Go on.

> Grace goes into the bedroom. Snake, still enjoying the music,
> takes a glance at her new writing.
> A scream—of joy. Grace comes back into the room,
> holding a pretty red dress.

Grace
You got it for me.

Snake
I was the first one in the store this morning.

Grace

Coming home from work I didn't see it in the window and
I thought someone else had got it.

> Grace stands in front of the tv,
> holding up the dress and styling. Feeling pretty.

Grace

Tv works pretty good as a mirror.

Snake

It looks great! I just wanted to thank you, for you know, for
inviting me.

Grace

And I want to thank you for accepting our invitation.
(Rest)
It'll work out. You'll see.

Snake

Let's see you in it. Try it on.

Grace

I can't keep it.

Snake

Sure you can.

Grace

No. Vet will—I can't keep it.
(Rest)
I'll put this on and Vet will see me in it. Then he'll get to
thinking. He's always thinking I'm running around on him.
Although I never did. But he's always thinking I did, or I do,
or I will. But I never did.

> She lays the dress aside,
> then starts putting away her Book and notes.

Snake

You'll finish your book some day.

Grace
Maybe.

Snake
You'll be on all the talk shows with it. They'll interview you in lots of magazines. And your Book, your Book, it'll be translated into all the languages.

Grace
Maybe.

> She continues stowing her Book and notes.

Grace
What's yours called? Your book?

Snake
The Book of Snake.

Grace
You might want to call it *The Book of Buddy.*

Snake
It's *The Book of Snake.*

Grace
Well. I'm proud of you.

Snake
Thanks.

Snake
Grace

(Rest)

> She finishes hiding her Book and notes.
> She holds the red dress, loving everything about it.
> Almost everything.

Grace
You'll return it?

Snake
I'll stow it away then return it tomorrow.

Grace
Ok.
(Rest)
I gotta get ready.

> Grace goes into the bathroom to take a shower.
> Snake turns up the radio, gets another beer, drinking it down.
> He takes the red dress. He looks toward his footlocker,
> then decides on a better hiding place. He tucks it underneath
> the floor with Grace's Book, then replaces the floor and the rug.
> Sounds of Grace in the shower.
> He takes up his phone, watching himself on playback.

Snake *(On playback)*
"When we strike against The Man, striking him at his
Ceremony, we will be careful, we will be smart. And after
we've struck him, and after we've wiped him out, we will
escape. We will move on. To the next target. He's just the
first of many."

> From the shower:

Grace
Once Vet gets his award, he'll feel like he's really
accomplished something. He'll be more into you working
with him, I'm telling you.

Snake
And I'm telling you I don't want to work with him.

Grace
Sure you do.

Snake
Sure I don't.

Grace

After the Ceremony it's all going to be better. I promise. You'll see.

> She comes out of the bedroom, wearing a bathrobe and slip,
> toweling her hair.

Snake

Don't go.

Grace

I'm going.
(Rest)
What's your book about?

Snake

Secret.

Grace

Tell me.

Snake

Take a look.

> Snake rewinds his video, finding a spot to show.

Snake *(On playback)*

"The Man likes keeping Us down. The Man has dug a hole for you, a hole in your yard with your name on it, and it's up to you to do something about that. Take some kind of action."

> He stops the video.

Grace

What kind of action?

Snake

Something big.

Grace

Like what?

Snake

It's a secret. I've got it all figured out. He's got it coming to
him. Strike One, Strike Two, Strike Three. 3-2-1—
You should stay home.

Grace

What are you going to do? Tell me.

Snake
Snake

Grace

Tell me.

> The sound of Vet's truck in the driveway.
> Snake gets another beer, opening it, drinking.

Grace

Buddy.

Snake

I'm Snake.

> Vet comes in. He surveys the situation:
> empty beer cans scattered around, the radio music blaring,
> Snake drinking a beer, and Grace, wearing a bathrobe and slip,
> her wet hair in a towel.

Vet
Grace
Snake

Grace

You're home. I'm almost ready. We were just celebrating.

Snake

We were celebrating *you*.

Vet

Is that what you're wearing?

Grace

Of course not. I'll get dressed.

Vet

Not yet. Let's celebrate.

> He gets a beer. Opens it. Drinks. Grace gets a beer.

Snake

To Pop.

Grace

Cheers.

Vet

You wearing that, kid?

Grace

Maybe you could put on a clean shirt.

Snake

I've got a suit coat.

> Snake goes to his footlocker, opening it. Grace tries to see inside,
> if he's hidden her dress there. Can't see.
> He takes out a wrinkled suit jacket.

Grace

Vet, you called me twice at work. To make sure I remembered
to get off early. And I did.
(Rest)
That's seen better days. I'll press it for you.

Vet

Let him do it.

> Snake sets up the ironing board, readies the iron.

Grace

A car's coming to pick us up. That's wonderful. Vet, that's
really great. They're sending a limousine.

Vet
It'll just be a car.

Grace
Still, we'll have a driver, right? That'll be something, right?
And there's a dinner afterwards. It's going to be really nice.

Snake
What's on the menu?

Vet
Steak. Potatoes.

Snake
Sounds great.

> Snake's ironing his jacket. Doing a pretty good job.

Grace
You're not nervous. But I'd be nervous. Having to talk in
front of all those people.

Vet
You and him can follow behind in the truck. You'd like that
better, right?

Grace
We'd like to ride with you.

Vet
You'll ride in the truck. With the kid. Ok?

Snake
Truck sounds great.

> Vet puts his truck keys on the table.

Grace
I should get changed.

Vet
Sit.

> She sits.
> Snake continues to iron his suit coat.
> Vet turns off the radio.

Vet
Vet
Grace
Snake
Vet
Vet

> The sound of Snake working the iron. Otherwise pretty quiet.

Vet
Grace
Vet

Vet
Snake
Grace
Vet

Vet
Look at him. Working the iron like his old man.

Vet
Grace
Snake
Vet

Vet
Snake
Grace
Vet

> Snake finishes and unplugs the iron. Vet sits.

Snake
Vet
Snake

> Snake goes to the fridge, getting another beer.
> Opening it. Drinking.

Vet
Snake
Vet

Snake
You should call for the time, Pop. Make sure we're on schedule.

> Vet, raging, grabs the house phone
> and throws it on the floor, breaking it.

Grace
Oh, the diner was crazy today. All those people in town for you. They had me running back and forth like a rat.

Vet
And when you came home you had to unwind.

Grace
We were celebrating you.

Vet
Celebrating? Right.

Snake
It's your big day, Pop

Grace
It's your big day, hon. We were celebrating.

Vet
That's the problem with letting things slide, Grace. I give you an inch and you slide a mile.

> Vet goes to Grace's hiding place, pulling away the rug.
> Snake starts toward him, then stops.

Vet
What? She's got something under here?

Snake

Who knows?

Vet

It took me a whole year to find out, but it took you just a day.

> Vet removes the floorboards, taking out Grace's Book.
> Then he finds the red dress. He takes it out, holding it up.

Grace

I bought it for *you*. So I could stand by your side and be your pretty wife.

Vet

So put it on.

> She takes the dress, heading toward the bedroom to change.

Vet

Stay. And put it on here.

Snake

Leave her lone, Pop.

Vet

Put it on right here. Go on.

Grace
Snake

> Snake turns his back, kindly giving her privacy
> and wishing he were anywhere but here.
> Grace puts on the dress as Vet speaks.

Vet

I work the Border Patrol it's a serious thing it's a daily struggle against the elements mind-melting heat blue-balling cold sunlight that'll blind you and darkness that'll make you want to lose your mind so you struggle daily against the elements and against the elements of your own

nature your nature and mine that's what I'm talking about
I am talking about Us and Them I am talking about keeping
the bad ones in line because it all comes down to Us and
Them you know what I'm talking about Us and Them it's
very clear it's very cut and dry it's very simple this over here
is ours and that over there is theirs over here I am an Us and
over here they are a Them but if we cross over to their side
suddenly we become a Them and they become an Us "why'd
you have to come here" I'd ask them I'm here because I live
here not like you the Fence it makes everything so clear
and if I had my way if I had my way hell we'd have more of
them we'd have a Fence in every city in every town in every
house because it makes things clear it tells me what I am
and what I'm standing for my way of life my own existence
and yours too because one slip could cause a downfall a
downfall for all of us on the job and at home too you are who
you are because I am who I am it's not that complicated to
understand.
(Rest)
That's my speech.

Grace now wears the red dress.

Grace
That's a nice speech, Vet. Do I look all right?

Vet examines her Book.

Grace
There's nothing bad in there. Nothing bad about you or
anybody. Let me keep it, Vet.

Snake
Leave her lone, Pop.

Vet
You two were intimate. I can tell.

Snake
Leave her lone, Pop.

Grace

We— Don't be silly, Vet. Don't be. Don't be—

> Vet starts ripping up her Book.
> Grace runs at him, and he shoves her away.

Snake

Leave her lone.

> Snake watching, like a child would watch.

Snake

Leave her lone, Pop.

> Vet dismembers her Book.

Grace

No! You keep me in a cage. Like I'm a dog. Or worse.

Snake

Leave her lone. Leave her lone. Leave her lone, Pop.

> She takes another run at Vet, again he shoves her away.

Grace

You don't let me do anything. You don't let me have anything.
You don't let me be anything. Except what you want. Which
is nothing. You want me to be just nothing. You dig a hole in
the yard for me? For what? I never did anything bad.

> Another run at Vet, again he shoves her.

Snake

Leave her lone, Pop. Please leave her lone.

Grace

I'm good but you treat me like I'm bad. And if I ever acted
bad, it'd be cause you drove me to it. Oh! That's what you
do. You drive everyone to bad. Look at me. Look at Buddy.
You drove him to bad just like you're driving me.

Vet
Did I drive you to bad?

Snake
Maybe.

Vet
How so?

Grace
Because of what you did to him. Something unspeakable.

Vet
Something unspeakable.

Grace
Yes.

Vet
Did I ever do anything "unspeakable" to you, Son?

Snake
Snake
Snake

> The Injustice, by its very nature,
> has moved just beyond the reach of words.
> And so Snake tries to speak
> but does not. Cannot.

Vet
See, Grace, I never did anything "unspeakable" to him.

> Vet gathers the ripped pages, plops them in a bucket.
> He takes some lighter fluid and douses them with it.

Grace
No, Vet, please. Lemmie keep it.

> Grace takes another run at him, again he shoves her.
> He lights a match. The pages burn.

Snake
I'm gonna wipe you out.

> Snake runs at Vet. Vet takes up the iron,
> raising it toward Snake. Grace intercedes.

Grace
Vet

(Rest)

Grace
Fuck you.

> With one swift stroke Vet hits Grace with the iron.
> She falls down dead.
> Snake goes to Grace, stops before reaching her.
> Vet douses the pages with water, stopping the fire
> and clearing away the smoke.

Snake
She's dead.

Vet
She's not your mother.

Snake
I know.

> Vet wipes off the iron. Regards Grace's body.

Vet
Help me.
(Rest)
Help me.

> The two men carry/drag Grace outside
> through the backdoor. Snake returns alone. He cries.
> Tears for himself, and for the whole world.

Snake

Snake

> As Vet comes back inside, Snake pulls himself together.
> Vet cleans himself up, quickly changing into his dress uniform,
> complete with gold braid. Holding his hat.
> Snake watches him.

Vet

Snake

Vet

Snake

Vet

She provoked me. It's her fault. I shouldn't of done it, but it's done. It's in the past. And whatever's between us, father and son, we'll work it out, starting right now. We'll work it out together. You're in this as much as me. You're the one who's got the blemishes on his record. You're the one they'll go after. But not to worry. I'll fix things so neither of us gets the blame.

> Vet's car for the Ceremony arrives. We hear it idling outside.

Vet

(Rest)

We're so much alike.

> Vet's finished dressing. Resplendent in his uniform. Ready to go.

Snake

I'm nothing like you.

Vet

Then why'd you have to come here? Huh? I moved out here to get a fresh start. And me and Grace, we were doing all right. We were doing great. I had it organized. And it was working great. And then you come visiting our home and you act like I never did anything good for you. Like I never gave you anything worth having. I gave you your life.

Snake
My life.

Vet
Yeah. That's something, right?

> Vet's car sounds its horn.

Vet
You can wear your medal, it's ok. You can show it off. You'll be a big deal, ok?

Snake
Yes, sir.

Vet
I can count on you?

Snake
Yes, sir.

Vet
Come ride with me.

Snake
I'll take the truck.

> Snake turns on the tv. Sounds of the marching band
> and local news reports of the Ceremony.

Snake
There they are getting ready for your Ceremony.

Vet
I'll see you there? Right?

Snake
You have my word. I'll be there.

> Vet goes.
> Snake takes out his phone and props it up.
> Turns it on self-video mode.

He goes to his footlocker. He takes out an empty
grenade-carrier vest and puts it on.
He removes the grenades from the footlocker,
putting them in the pockets of his vest. He puts his medal
in his pocket too, then turns the tv off.
He speaks into his phone, finishing his book.

Snake

The Book of Snake, New Chapter: A Change in Plan. Because
I am The Man. I'm a part of him, anyway.
(Rest)
He gave me my life. Ok. And so I'll take it away. Ok. I'll
take away his and I'll take away mine, his and mine both
together. I'll take it all away. And you'll watch this here
when I'm gone, and then you'll know.
(Rest)
[[When in the course of human events it becomes necessary
ok for a people ok to dissolve the bands which have
connected them with another ok—
(Rest)
We hold these truths to be self-evident, that all men are
created equal, that they are endowed by their Creator
with certain unalienable rights, that among these are Life,
Liberty and the Pursuit of Happiness. Ok. Whatever.
(Rest)
Whenever or whatever form becomes destructive to these
ends, it is the right of the people to alter or abolish it.
(Rest)
When a long train of abuses is designed to reduce us, it is
our right, it is our duty, to throw off such.
(Rest)
He has refused to Assent to Laws
(Rest)
He has protected himself from punishment for any Murders
(Rest)
He has excited Domestic Insurrections amongst us
(Rest)
Our repeated petitions have been answered only by repeated
injury. I therefore pledge my life, my fortune and my sacred
honor.]]

The backdoor opens. After a moment, Grace comes inside.
Walking slowly. Dirt spills off her. From her face
and hands and hair. From the creases of her dress and body.
The dirt leaves a trail into the house. She stumbles,
catches herself, runs her fingers through her hair,
touches her face, coughs, stops.
Snake watches her.

Snake
I thought you were—

Grace
Dead. No.

She looks at her Book, its pages mostly all burned.
At last she notices Snake. Dressed in his bombs.

Snake
Grace
Snake
Grace

(Rest)

She brushes absently at her clothing.
She coughs. More and more coughing for an uncomfortable
amount of time. She gets water, douses her Book.
Snake watches.
She gathers up her Book, torn and burned.

Grace
Grace
Grace

Grace
Snake
Grace
Snake

Snake
I'm going to the Fence.

Grace
Don't.

Snake
You can call for help if you want.

> He moves toward the door.
> Grace takes a page, reading from it.

Grace
"The Magic Castle . . . After all those years . . ."

> He stops.
> Another page, another fragment.

Grace
"One of my hopes involves . . . I work . . . I've put my name on it . . . it's mine . . ."

> Another page, another fragment.

Grace
". . . made in India or made in China or made . . ."

> More pages, more fragments.

Grace
"Today I'm feeling like . . . Gold st—"
(Rest)
"The House of Wisdom . . ."
(Rest)
"Javier . . . Japanese."

> More pages, more fragments.

Grace
"Charlotte's daughter Charlotte . . . about as big as she is . . ."
(Rest)
". . . The lake where we all jumped in . . ."

> Another page. Another fragment.

Grace
"And then that Trouble headed off . . ."
(Rest)
"He never told me . . . So I make it up."

Not reading now, just talking.

Grace
Like, like, like, like maybe, one day, Will comes home. And the dog's there. Just sitting on the porch. After all those years.

Snake
Tell me that part again.

Grace
What part.

Snake
The part you made up.

Grace
Snake
Grace

She faces him and extends her hand.
He takes a step toward her.
Perhaps even another.
Then he stops.
And they might just stay like that forever.

Grace
Snake
Grace

A bell, thumb-cymbal sounding, rings.

End of Play

Named one of *TIME* magazine's "100 Innovators for the Next New Wave," in 2002 Suzan-Lori Parks became the first African-American woman to receive the Pulitzer Prize in Drama for her Broadway hit *Topdog/Underdog*. A MacArthur "Genius" Fellowship recipient, she has also been awarded grants by the National Endowment for the Arts, the Rockefeller Foundation, the Ford Foundation, the New York State Council on the Arts and the New York Foundation for the Arts. She is the recipient of a Lila Wallace–Reader's Digest Award, a CalArts/Herb Alpert Award in the Arts (Theatre) for 1996, a Guggenheim Foundation Fellowship and the 2015 Dorothy & Lillian Gish Prize. She is an alumna of Mount Holyoke College and New Dramatists.

Her numerous plays include *Father Comes Home from the Wars (Parts 1, 2 & 3)* (2015 Pulitzer Prize finalist, 2015 Edward M. Kennedy Prize for Drama Inspired by American History, 2014 Horton Foote Prize), *The Book of Grace*, *Topdog/Underdog* (2002 Pulitzer Prize), *In the Blood* (2000 Pulitzer Prize finalist), *Venus* (1996 OBIE Award), *The Death of the Last Black Man in the Whole Entire World*, *Fucking A*, *Imperceptible Mutabilities in the Third Kingdom*

(1990 OBIE Award for Best New American Play) and *The America Play*. Parks's work on *The Gershwins' Porgy and Bess* earned the production a Tony Award for Best Revival of a Musical in 2012. In 2007 her *365 Days/365 Plays* was produced in more than seven hundred theaters worldwide, creating one of the largest grassroots collaborations in theater history. Her work is the subject of the PBS film *The Topdog Diaries*.

Park's first novel, *Getting Mother's Body*, was published by Random House in 2003.

Her first short film, *Anemone Me*, was assistant-directed by Todd Haynes and produced by Christine Vachon. Her first feature-length screenplay, *Girl 6*, was written for Spike Lee. She has also written numerous screenplays, including the adaptation of Zora Neale Hurston's classic novel *Their Eyes Were Watching God*, which premiered on ABC's Oprah Winfrey Presents. As a film actor, Parks has also appeared in the fictional-documentary *The Making of Plus One*, which premiered at the Cannes Film Festival in 2009.

In November 2008 Parks became the first recipient of the Master Writer Chair at The Public Theater. At The Public, and as she tours the country, she performs her innovative performance piece, *Watch Me Work*, a play with action and dialogue/a meta-theatrical writing class. She also serves as a visiting arts professor in dramatic writing at New York University's Tisch School of the Arts.

Holding honorary doctorates from Brown University, among others, Parks credits her writing teacher and mentor, James Baldwin, for starting her on the path of playwriting. One of the first to recognize Parks's writing skills, Mr. Baldwin declared Parks "an astonishing and beautiful creature who may become one of the most valuable artists of our time."